D0100059

My First Animal Kingdom Encyclopedias

ARACHNIDS

by Pamela Dell

Consultant: Jackie Gai, DVM
Wildlife Veterinarian

CAPSTONE PRESS
a capstone imprint

A+ Books are published by Capstone Press,
1710 Roe Crest Drive, North Mankato, Minnesota 56003
www.mycapstone.com

Library of Congress Cataloging-in-Publication Data is available on the Library of
Congress website.
ISBN 978-1-5157-3924-1 (library binding)
ISBN 978-1-5157-3934-0 (paperback)
ISBN 978-1-5157-3964-7 (eBook PDF)

Summary: A photo-illustrated reference guide to arachnids that highlights physical features,
diet, life cycles, and more.

Editorial Credits

Kathryn Clay, editor; Rick Korab and Juliette Peters, designers;
Kelly Garvin, media researcher; Gene Bentdahl, production specialist

Photo Credits

Alamy/Andrew Mackay, 30 (top left), Getty Images: BSIP/Contributor, 23 (top), Patrick
AVENTURIER, 31 (top right); Minden Pictures: Piotr Naskrecki, 26 (middle), Stephen Dalton,
16 (tr), 17 (b), 18 (bottom left), Newscom: Avinash Harpude/NHPA/Photoshot, 28 (right),
Corey Hochachka/Design Pics, 19 (bl), Science Source: Stephen Dalton, 21 (r), Tom McHugh,
15 (t), Shutterstock: Aleksey Stemmer, 17 (tr), Amith Nag, 5, Anatolich, 6-7, Ang Kean Leng,
25 (b), Arnold John Labrentz, 31 (bottom right), AquaFotoZen, 12 (bottom), backpacker79, 32,
basel101658, back cover, 12-13, Bruce MacQueen, 26 (b), Cathy Keifer, cover (bl), 8 (m), cyrrpit,
30 (bl), D. Kucharski K. Kucharska, 12 (t), Daniel Szymanski, 8 (t), Dannis van de Water, 30 (tr),
Dave Rock, 11 (tl), Dennis W Donohue, 26-27, Dr. Morley Read, 11 (bl), 25 (t), 29 (tl), Dray van
Beeck, 13 (b), Erik Karits, 1 (left), 22 (tr), ex0rzist, 17 (tl), Fabio Maffei, 24-25, Galinago_media,
24 (b), Henrik Artur Janichev, cover (tr), IrinaK, 1 (tr), 20 (b), Ivan Kuzmin, 26 (t), Katarina
Christenson, 27 (t), Kletr, 9 (t), Larsson, cover (tl), LFRabanedo, 10-11, llvutchenko Galina, 18-19,
LorraineHudgins, 14 (t), magnetix, 18 (br), Maksimilian, 10 (l),Maria Jeffs, 28-29, MarkMirror,
8 (b), 19 (br), Mikhail Egorov, 21 (l), Milan Vachal, 31 (bl), Neil Burton 22-23, Nik Br, 8-9, Pan
Xunbin, 24 (t), papkin, 16 (l), Pavel Krasensky, 9 (b), 13 (t), 31 (tl), Phumjai Fc, 1 (middle right),
Robyn Bulter, 16 (mr), Ryan M. Bolton, 11 (top middle), Sari ONeal, 16 (br), 28 (l), Sebastian
Janicki, 4-5, shaftinaction, 12 (m), SIMON SHIM, 30 (br), South 12th Photography, 29 (tr), Steven
Ellingson, 14 (b), 23 (b), 29 (b), stevenku, 15 (b), Sutipong Arsirapoj, cover (br), Tomatito, 16-17,
tose, 11 (tr), v.gi, 22 (b), Valik, 2-3 (bkg), VICHAILAO, cover, 1 (bkg), Vinokurov Kirill, 14-15,
violart, 4, Vova Shevchuk, 20-21, yingphoto, 22 (tl), zaidi razak, 9 (m), zstock, 11 (br),
Wikimedia/Jaroslav Smrž, Lubomír Kovác, Jaromír Mikeš, Alena Lukešová, 25 (m)

Artistic elements: Shutterstock: Decent, fxmdusan73, Gallinago_media,
Kazakov Makism, Valik, VICHAILAO

TABLE OF CONTENTS

What Are Arachnids?

Arachnids are a group of small, eight-legged animals. Spiders are the most well known. But there are 10 other orders of arachnids. These orders include scorpions, ticks, and mites.

class
a smaller group of living things; arachnids are in the class Arachnida

kingdom
one of five very large groups into which all living things are placed; the two main kingdoms are plants and animals; arachnids belong to the animal kingdom

phylum
(FIE-lum)
a group of living things with a similar body plan; arachnids belong to the phylum Arthropoda (ar-THROP-uh-duh); insects and crustaceans are also in this group

order
a group of living things that is smaller than a class; there are 11 orders of arachnids alive today

arthropod
(AR-thruh-pod)
an invertebrate with
many body sections;
crustaceans, insects,
and spiders are
arthropods

invertebrate
(in-VUR-tuh-brit)
an animal without a
backbone; arachnids,
insects, and worms
are invertebrates

cold-blooded
also called
ectothermic
(EK-tuh-THER-mik)
cold-blooded animals have
a body temperature that is
the same as the air around
them; arachnids are
cold-blooded

species
(SPEE-sees)
a group of animals
that are alike and can
produce young with each
other; there are more
than 70,000 species
of arachnids

araneae
(uh-RAY-nee-ay)
the special group of
arachnids that includes
all spiders

Part by Part

Arachnids have two main body parts and many smaller parts. The head and thorax make up one main part. The other main part is the abdomen.

chitin
(KIE-tin)
the material that makes up the exoskeleton

exoskeleton
(EK-so-SKEL-ih-ton)
the hard covering that protects the inner parts of animals without backbones; all arachnids have exoskeletons

leg
a limb on which an animal stands; all arachnids have eight legs attached to the thorax

mouthpart
a small limb or structure around the mouth; fangs and strong jaws are mouthparts used for cutting, chewing, stabbing, and sucking

abdomen
(AB-duh-muhn)
the thick back part of the body on most arachnids; the abdomen holds a spider's silk and lungs

thorax
(THOR-aks)
part of an arachnid's body; the thorax is connected to the head

head
a part of the body that holds the brain and sensing organs

pedipalp
(PED-uh-palp)
a body part that looks like an extra leg near the jaws; pedipalps are used for grabbing or sensing

7

From Egg to Adult

Young arachnids already look much like adults. Besides growing larger, they change very little.

larva

(LAR-vuh): an arachnid that has hatched from its egg

life cycle

the series of changes that take place in a living thing, from birth to death; the life cycle for all arachnids starts with an egg

life span

the number of years a certain animal usually lives; most spiders live about one year; some scorpions can live 15 years

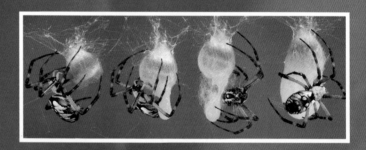

egg

most arachnids lay their eggs in a brood sac; scorpions carry their eggs inside their bodies, then give birth to live young

brood sac

also called an egg sac; a small, silk bundle made by a female spider to hold and keep her eggs safe

spiderling
a very young spider

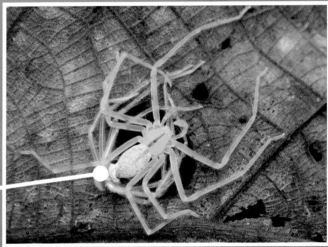

molt
to shed; when arachnids get too big
for their exoskeleton, they crawl
out of it; the old one is replaced by
a larger one; spiders may molt up to
12 times during their lifetime

nymph
(NIMF): a young arachnid that has
molted at least once

At Home on Land

Arachnids live in almost every habitat on Earth. Some arachnids live in cold places. But many like warm places best.

desert
(DEH-zuhrt): a dry area that gets little rain; many scorpions live in the desert

habitat
the type of place and conditions in which a plant or animal lives; arachnids live in many different habitats, including rain forests, deserts, and the tundra

tundra
(TUN-druh): a large, flat area of land found in the Arctic; no trees grow in the tundra, and the ground is always frozen; more than 100 species of spiders live in the tundra

tropics
a hot, humid part of the world near the equator; many arachnids live in the tropics

arboreal

(ar-BOR-ee-uhl): having to do with trees; many tarantulas are arboreal, making their homes in trees

cave

a large hole formed underground or on the side of a cliff or hill; Kauai cave wolf spiders live in caves on the Hawaiian island of Kauai

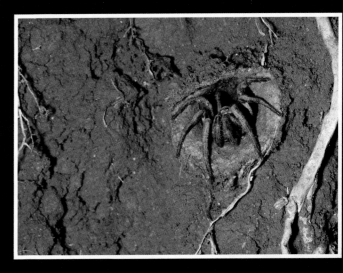

rain forest

a thick area of trees where rain falls almost every day; about 3,600 species of spiders live in the Amazon rain forest

burrow

a tunnel or hole in the ground made or used by an animal; trapdoor spiders weave doors for their burrows; when insects walk by, the spider pushes the trapdoor open and grabs them

At Home in the Water

Arachnids don't live only on land. Some spend part or all of their time in water.

shrimp
some water spiders eat shrimp; they blow bubbles around the shrimp to trap them

freshwater
water that does not contain salt; most ponds, rivers, lakes, and streams are freshwater bodies

aquatic
(a-KWA-dik)
relating to animals that live in water; water mites are aquatic

fishing spider
also called a raft spider; these arachnids sit at the water's edge and wait to feel ripples in the water from a nearby fish; they then grab the fish with hooks on their front legs

wind
fishing spiders use the wind to help them move across the water; they can also walk across the surface of the water

air bubble
diving bell spiders spin webs under the water's surface; they collect air bubbles underneath the web and use them to breathe underwater

sea spider
though they look like spiders, sea spiders are not true spiders; they belong to the same phylum as arachnids, but not the same class

Let's Eat

Nearly all arachnids are meat-eaters. They either hunt for their food or feed off animals that are already dead.

predator
(PRED-uh-tur)
an animal that hunts other animals for food; except for some mites, all arachnids are predators

carnivore
(KAHR-nuh-vor)
an animal that eats only meat; arachnids feed mostly on insects

parasite
an animal or plant that lives on or inside another animal or plant; ticks are parasites; they live on the blood of birds and mammals

prey
(PRAY): an animal hunted by other animals for food; small rodents, such as mice, are sometimes prey for larger spiders

scavenger
(SKAV-in-jer): an animal that feeds on animals that are already dead; dust mites feed on dead skin cells

15

Spotlight on Spiders

There are about 40,000 known spider species. They live everywhere in the world except Antarctica.

ballooning
a way for young and very small spiders to travel through the air; the spider spins a line of silk and "flies" on the end of it

arachnophobia
(uh-RAK-nuh-FOH-bee-uh)
the fear of spiders

net-casting spiders
spiders that spin a thick, postage stamp-sized web and drop it on top of their prey

silk
the thread that spiders make inside their bodies; spiders use silk to wrap up insects to eat and to make egg sacs; sticky silk is used to build webs

venom
(VEN-uhm)
a poison that some animals make; only a few spiders have venom strong enough to hurt people

spitting spiders

a group of spiders that spit venomous silk at their prey; the glue-like venom covers the prey

tarantula

(tuh-RAN-chuh-luh): a large, hairy spider; tarantulas live mostly in warm areas, such as South America, Australia, and the southwestern United States

jumping spiders

a spider family that includes more than 4,000 species; some jumping spiders can jump 25 times farther than the length of their own bodies

What a Web!

Not all spiders spin webs. But those that do sure work hard! Some spiders weave webs with beautiful designs. These webs are used to catch insects and other prey.

trap line

a silk thread that moves when something gets caught in the web; the movement tells the spider that dinner might be waiting

spinneret

(spin-uh-RET): also called a spinner; the small body part that shoots out the threads spiders use to build their webs

silk gland

the part of a spider's body that stores silk-making liquid

spiral

a twisty, coil shape; some spiders weave spiral webs that grow smaller as they reach the center of the web

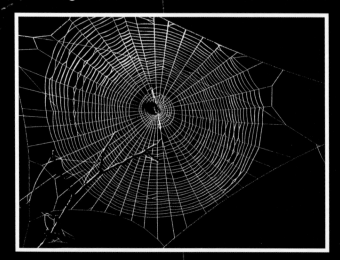

orb
a round shape; spiders that spin round webs are called orb weavers

tube web
purseweb spiders build a silky tube; the tube is partly above ground and partly underground; the spider hides in the tube and waits for prey

megaweb
a huge spiderweb made by many spiders spinning webs that connect together; sometimes millions of spiders work together to create megawebs

19

The Scoop on Scorpions

Scorpions are arachnids with lobster-like claws. Their long tails curve up and forward. The tails have a stinger at the tip.

metasoma
(MET-uh-SO-mah)
another name for a scorpion's tail; the metasoma has six sections; the end section holds venom

nocturnal
(nok-TUR-nuhl)
active at night; many scorpions hide underground during the day; they search for food at night

giant desert hairy scorpion
the largest scorpion in North America; these arachnids get their name from the brown hairs that cover their body

pincers
also called chelae (KEE-lee); another name for a scorpion's claw-like pedipalps; scorpions use their pincers to grab and hold prey

stinger
also called
an aculeus
(uh-KYOO-lee-uhs);
the needle-like part that
sticks out at the end of a
scorpion's tail; stingers
are used to attack prey
and inject venom

**deathstalker
scorpion**
one of the deadliest
scorpions; it surprises its
prey with a quick, painful
sting; deathstalkers live in
northern Africa and the
Middle East

hibernate
(HYE-bur-nate)
to spend the winter
months in a deep
sleep; scorpions that
live in colder
places hibernate

Mighty Mites and Ticks

Mites and ticks are some of the smallest arachnids. Many of them cannot be seen without a microscope!

hard tick
a tick with a hard shell; all ticks are either hard-shelled or soft-shelled

soft tick
a tick that does not have a hard shell; soft ticks look wrinkled, much like raisins

host
a plant or animal on which a parasite lives

questing
the position of a hard tick waiting for a host; a questing tick stands on the edge of a leaf or grass stem; it sticks out its legs and waits for a host to pass by

microscopic
(my-kruh-SKOP-ik) so small it can be seen only under a microscope or magnifying glass; most mites are microscopic

chigger
a young mite; like ticks, chiggers are parasites; bites from these tiny red bugs may cause itching and redness

acari
(AK-uh-rye) the group of arachnids to which mites and ticks belong

red velvet mite
also called a rain bug; red velvet mites come out after a rain to feed; they're often mistaken for spiders

23

Other Arachnids

Spiders, scorpions, and mites and ticks make up the three most common orders of arachnids. But many other kinds of arachnids exist.

vinegaroons
another name for whip scorpions; vinegaroons can spray a vinegar-like liquid to keep themselves safe from predators

pseudoscorpions
(SOO-doh-SCORE-pe-uhnz): arachnids that look much like small, tailless scorpions; "pseudo" means false or fake; lacking tails, pseudoscorpions store venom in their claws

tailless whip scorpions
also called cave spiders; they are neither spider nor scorpion

microwhip scorpions
a little-known type of tiny arachnid; the biggest microwhip scorpions are just 0.1 inch (2.5 millimeters) long

split-middle whip scorpions
also called short-tailed whip scorpions; arachnids whose head and thorax are split in the middle, forming two hard plates

whip scorpions
small arachnids that look like scorpions with long, thin whip-like tails; whip scorpions use their two front legs as feelers

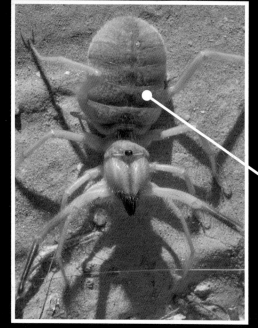

sun spiders

also called wind scorpions, camel spiders, and beardcutters; these arachnids move fast and have giant, dangerous-looking jaws; the largest sun spiders measure 6 inches (15 centimeters) long

hooded tick spiders

tiny arachnids that are neither ticks nor spiders; hooded tick spiders have poor eyesight and usually live in damp soil

hood

a hard but moveable part of a hooded tick spider's exoskeleton; the hood can move up and down to cover the arachnid's mouthparts

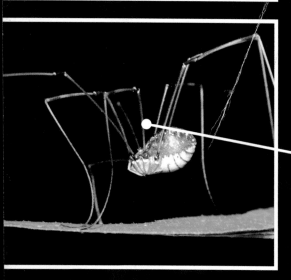

harvestmen

also called daddy longlegs; harvestmen have only two eyes and no fangs or venom; their body has only one section

whip spiders

like whip scorpions, whip spiders
use their long front legs as feelers;
whip spiders have no tails; their flat
bodies are broken into sections

Dangerous Creatures

They bite! They sting! They spread disease! Watch out for these arachnids.

Indian red scorpion
this arachnid measures just 2 to 3.5 inches (5–9 cm) long, but its venom is deadly; no known anti-venom works well against it

black widow
a black spider with a red hourglass-shaped mark on its underside; a black widow's venom is 15 times stronger than rattlesnake venom

neurotoxin
(NOOR-oh-tok-sin)
a strong poison in a wood tick's saliva; the neurotoxin makes the tick's host unable to move

Brazilian wandering spider

also called the banana spider because it's often found on banana plants; thought to be the world's most venomous spider

Rocky Mountain wood tick

its bite can cause Rocky Mountain spotted fever; the first symptom is usually a red, non-itchy rash

deer tick

lives in grassy or wooded areas; a bite from a young deer tick (nymph) can spread Lyme disease; deer tick nymphs look like poppy seeds

anti-venom

a medicine that helps people get better after being bitten by a venomous animal

Fun Facts

The **Darwin's bark spider** weaves the world's largest webs. Some webs are as long as two city buses.

Spiny orb weaver spiders are also known as horned spiders. Pointy horns, or spines, stick out from their bodies. The horns scare away predators.

The **Goliath bird-eating tarantula** has a leg span of up to 12 inches (30 cm). It injects venom into birds with its 1-inch (2.5-cm) fangs.

The **bird dung crab spider** is not very pretty. It looks and smells like a pile of bird poop.

The **diving bell spider** spends its entire life underwater.

The world's oldest **microwhip scorpion** was discovered in Myanmar. No bigger than a grain of rice, its body had been trapped in a piece of tree sap. The tiny arachnid lived 100 million years ago.

In ultraviolet light, **scorpions** have a light-blue body. Special chemicals in their hard outer shell make them glow.

The markings on the **happy face spider** often look like a face with a big, smiling mouth.

READ MORE

McFadzean, Lesley. *Insects*. Discovery Education. Animals. New York: PowerKids Press, 2015.

Owings, Lisa. *From Egg to Honeybee*. Start to Finish, Second Series. Minneapolis: Lerner Publications, 2016.

Rustad, Martha E. H. *Insects*. Smithsonian Little Explorer. Little Scientist. North Mankato, Minn.: Capstone Press, a Capstone imprint, 2015.

INTERNET SITES

FactHound offers a safe, fun way to find Internet sites related to this book. All of the sites on FactHound have been researched by our staff.

Here's all you do:
Visit *www.facthound.com*
Type in this code:
9781515739241

Super-cool stuff!

Check out projects, games and lots more at
www.capstonekids.com